ADVANTAGE Reading 1

Table of Contents

Table of Contents

CREDITS

Concept Development: Kent Publishing Services, Inc.
Written by: Beth Sycamore
Editor: Carla Hamaguchi
Designer/Production: Moonhee Pak/Terri Lamadrid
Illustrator: Jenny Campbell
Art Director: Tom Cochrane
Project Director: Carolea Williams

Introduction

The Advantage Reading Series for grades K-2 is shaped and influenced by current research findings in literacy instruction grounded in the federally mandated *No Child Left Behind* Act. It includes the following five key skill strands:

- phonemic awareness
- phonics/structural word analysis
- vocabulary development
- reading fluency
- reading comprehension

This series offers strong skill instruction along with motivational features in an easy-to-use format.

Take a look at all the advantages this reading series offers . . .

Varied Reading Selections

Fiction and Nonfiction

Meaningful reading experiences are offered across a **variety of reading genres.** Each story selection builds on high-frequency words, content vocabulary, and skills introduced in the section. The reading selection at the end of each unit can be removed from the workbook and folded into a mini-book.

Graphic Information

Graphic information reading selections include charts, graphs, labels, maps, and recipes. These types of reading opportunities help students hone **real-life reading** skills.

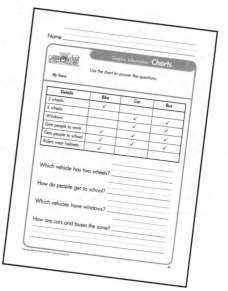

Introduction

High-Frequency Words

A word list is included for an overview of the words a student should easily recognize at each grade level and that are used in the reading selections throughout the workbook. For extra practice, prepare flashcards of the words on the list for students to practice recognizing and reading quickly. This will help students develop a solid bank of **sight words on which they can rely and that are automatic.**

Fluency Practice

Reading fluency is the ability to **read with expression,** intonation, and a natural flow that sounds like talking. Fluency is essential for comprehension because the lack of it results in choppy, robotic reading that stands in the way of making sense out of a phrase or sentence.

Writing

Reading and writing are partner skills. Students are given opportunities to transfer their newly learned reading skills to **authentic writing** opportunities.

Extensions and Real-Life Applications

Each unit ends with a "More Things to Do" page that includes suggestions for **hands-on experiences** that extend the theme. A list of books is also included for further study and enjoyment of the unit's theme.

Answer Key

Pages, with the answers completed, are reproduced in a miniature format at the back of the book to make **checking answers quick and easy.**

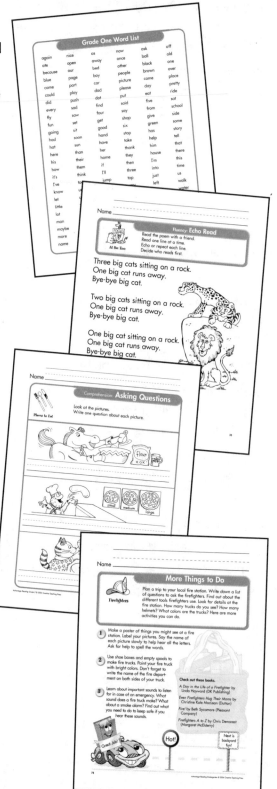

Grade One Word List

again	nice	as	now	ask	off
ate	open	away	once	ball	old
because	our	bed	other	black	one
blue	page	boy	people	brown	over
came	part	car	picture	come	place
could	play	dad	please	day	pretty
did	push	dot	put	eat	ride
every	sad	find	said	five	sat
fly	saw	four	say	from	school
fun	set	get	shop	give	side
going	sit	good	six	green	some
had	soon	hand	stop	has	story
hat	sun	have	take	help	tell
here	than	her	thank	him	that
his	their	home	they	house	there
how	them	if	then	I'm	this
it's	think	I'll	three	into	time
I've	too	jump	top	just	us
know	under	last	very	left	walk
let	use	letter	want	like	water
little	was	live	well	look	were
lot	way	love	went	make	when
man	what	many	white	may	who
maybe	where	men	why	might	words
more	will	mother	with	must	yellow
name	yes	new	you'll	next	zoo

5

How to Make the Mini-Books

1 Tear out the page.

2 Cut along the dashed line.

3 Fold both sections along the fold line.

4 Insert the middle section.

Name _____

In My Neighborhood

Comprehension: Prior Knowledge

There are many things to see in a neighborhood.
Draw a map of your neighborhood.
Think about people, places, and things to see.
Use words to label your picture.

Name _____

In My Neighborhood

Name the pictures.
Circle the pictures whose names rhyme.

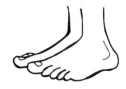      

Draw a picture of something that rhymes with  .

Advantage Reading Grade 1 © 2004 Creative Teaching Press

Name _____

In My Neighborhood

Name the pictures.
Color the boxes to show how many sounds you hear.

I hear two sounds in  .

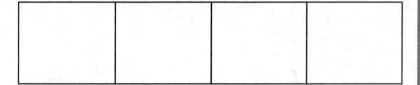

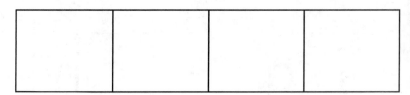

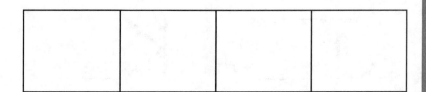

Name _____

In My Neighborhood

Write the matching letter.

A ____   B ____   C ____

____ d   ____ e   F ____

____ g   ____ h   I ____

J ____   K ____   L ____

M ____   ____ n   ____ o

Name _____

Capital and Lowercase Letters

In My Neighborhood

Write the matching letter.

P _ _ _ _ _   q   R _ _ _ _

S _ _ _ _ _   T _ _ _ _   _ _ u

V _ _ _ _ _   W _ _ _ _   _ _ x

_ _ y   Z _ _ _ _

Write three capital and lowercase letters that look the same.

 C c _ _ _ _ _ _ _ _ _ _ _ _ _ _

_ _ _ _ _ _ _ _ _ _ _ _ _ _

Name _____

In My Neighborhood

Name the picture.
Write the letter that makes the beginning sound.

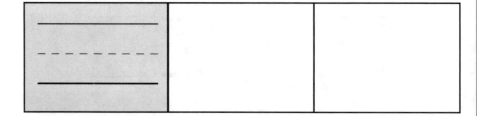

Name _____

In My Neighborhood

Name the picture.
Write the letter that makes the ending sound.

		____ ____ ____
		____ ____ ____
		____ ____ ____
		____ ____ ____
		____ ____ ____

Name _____

In My Neighborhood

Circle three letters in the box.
Write words that begin with each letter.

h	r	m	n	w
s	t	p	g	d

Write a name for a person.

_____

_____

Write a name for a place.

_____

_____

Write a name for a thing.

_____

_____

Use one of your words to write a sentence.

_____

_____

     Advantage Reading Grade 1 © 2004 Creative Teaching Press

Name _____

In My Neighborhood

Read the tongue twister.
Answer the questions.

Four fast firemen with funny faces

Read it again.
How will you read it?   (Fast)   (Slow)

Read it again.
How will you read it?   (Big voice)   (Little voice)

Read it again.
How many Ffs can you count?   _____

_____

Name _____

In My Neighborhood

Write words that tell about places in your neighborhood.

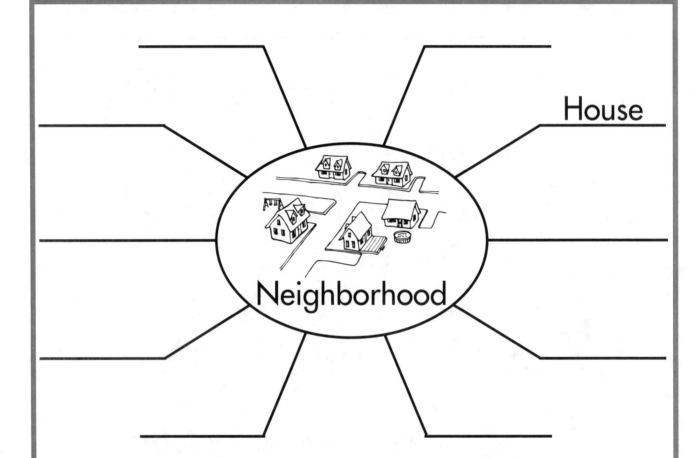

House

Neighborhood

Use some of the words to write about your neighborhood.

_____

_____

_____

_____

Name _____

In My Neighborhood

Read the words in the box.
Use the words to complete the sentences.

the	to	on	go

I _____ to the park.

We ride _____ a bus.

I like _____ play.

Where is _____ slide?

Name _____

In My Neighborhood

Read the words in the box.
Choose one day of the week.
Write and draw what happened to you on that day.

Monday Tuesday Wednesday Thursday Friday Saturday Sunday

Read the words again. Write the day of the week that has three beats.

_____

_____

Off We Go

1

We go to the pool on Tuesday.

3

Fold
Here

We stay home on Sunday.

8

We go to the zoo on Friday.

6

2 We go to the pet store on Monday.

4 We go to the post office on Wednesday.

Fold
Here

We go to the park on Saturday.

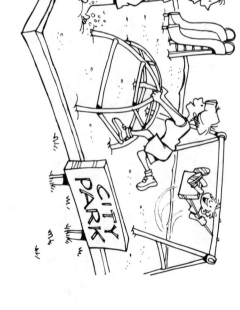

7

We go to the library on Thursday.

5

Name _____

In My Neighborhood

Think about the book *Off We Go.*
Draw pictures that tell where the characters went.
Use your pictures to retell the story to a friend.

Monday

Tuesday

Wednesday

Thursday

Friday

Saturday

Sunday

Name _____

In My Neighborhood

Use the letters to make three words.

e	h	o	m

This word describes a place to live.

Advantage Reading Grade 1 © 2004 Creative Teaching Press

Name _____

In My Neighborhood

Look at the chart.
Use the chart to answer the questions.

Sign Shapes

⬡	△	▭	◇
||||	||	|	|||

How many ⬡ signs? _____

How many ▭ signs? _____

How many △ signs? _____

How many ◇ signs? _____

Draw a sign
you see in your
neighborhood.

Name _____

In My Neighborhood

Everyone can help in a neighborhood.
How do you take care of your neighborhood?
Draw a picture and write about what you do.

Name _____

More Things to Do

In My Neighborhood

You can learn about letters and words anytime! Talk about letters and words you see around your school or neighborhood. Trace the letters you find, say the letter names, or say the sound of a letter you know in a word. Talk about people, places, and things you see. Choose one or two activities from below to complete.

1. Make an ABC Neighborhood Book. Write a word and draw a picture for each letter of the alphabet.

2. Find and circle letters in a newspaper or advertisement.

3. Make a list of people who help out in the neighborhood. Describe each person's special job.

4. Create a picture map of the buildings on your street. Write the names and phone numbers of your neighbors.

Check out these books.

I Read Signs by Tana Hoban
   (Greenwillow Books)

The Jolly Postman and Other People's Letters
   by Janet and Allan Ahlberg
   (Little, Brown and Company)

My Perfect Neighborhood by Leah Komaiko
   (HarperCollins)

Wake Up, City! by Alvin Tresselt
   (Lothrop Lee & Shepard)

Hooray!

Yeah!

The next stop is the zoo.

Name

At the Zoo

There are many things to see at a zoo.
Complete the chart.
Add words that describe things you might see.

Animals	Buildings	People

What question would you ask a zookeeper?

Name _____

At the Zoo

Name the pictures.
Draw a line to match pictures whose names have the same beginning sound.

Draw two pictures that have the same beginning sound as .

Name _____

Name the pictures.
Draw a line to match pictures whose names have the same ending sound.

Draw two pictures that have the same ending sound as  .

Name _____

At the Zoo

Use the letters in the box to make words with **short a**.

m	r	c

_____ at

_____ at

_____ at

_____ an

_____ an

_____ an

Read your words. Write a word that names a pet.

_____

Name _____

At the Zoo

Use the letters in the box to make words with **short e**.

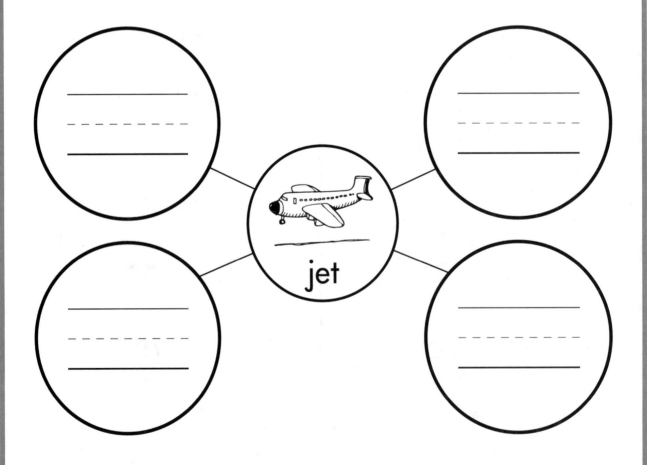

Read your words. Write a word that names something used to catch fish.

_____
_____
_____

Name _____

At the Zoo

Follow the directions to make words with **short i**.

Write the word ⑥. ___ ___ ___

Change the first letter to make a new word. ___ i x

Change the last letter to make a new word. s i ___

Write all your words.

_____

_ _

_____

Write the word 🐷. ___ ___ ___

Change the first letter to make a new word. ___ ig

Change the last letter to make a new word. p i ___

Write all your words.

_____

_ _

_____

Name _____

At the Zoo

Use the letters in the box to make words with **short o**.

h	t	j	l	m

_____ og

_____ og

_____ og

_____ op

_____ op

_____ op

Read your words. Write a word
that names a toy.

_____

           Advantage Reading Grade 1 © 2004 Creative Teaching Press

Name _____

Use the letters in the box to make words with **short u**.

j	r	h	b

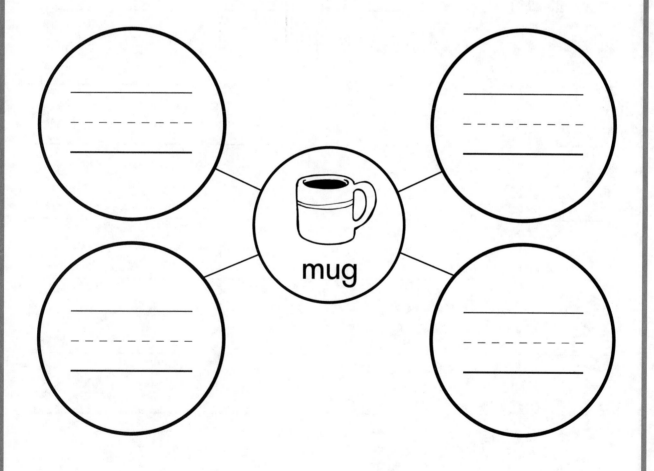

mug

Read your words. Write a word that names something small.

_____

_____

_____

Name _____

At the Zoo

Phonics: **Short Vowel Words**

Name each picture.
Write the missing letter.
Use the spelling pattern to write a new word.

____ an   ____ an   ____ ____ ____

____ et   ____ et   ____ ____ ____

____ ig   ____ ig   ____ ____ ____

____ op   ____ op   ____ ____ ____

____ ug   ____ ug   ____ ____ ____

Name _____

At the Zoo

Fluency: Echo Read

Read the poem with a friend.
Read one line at a time.
Echo or repeat each line.
Decide who reads first.

Three big cats sitting on a rock.
One big cat runs away.
Bye-bye big cat.

Two big cats sitting on a rock.
One big cat runs away.
Bye-bye big cat.

One big cat sitting on a rock.
One big cat runs away.
Bye-bye big cat.

No more big cats!

Read it again.
Use your hands to show the actions.
How will you show the big cats resting?
How will you show the big cats running away?

Name _____

At the Zoo

Look at each pair of pictures.
Draw what might happen next.

Name _____

At the Zoo

Read the words in the box.
Use the words to complete the sentences.

is	an	with	zoo

I went on a trip _____ my dad.

We went to the _____.

Where _____ the monkey house?

There is _____ alligator.

Name _____

At the Zoo

Read the words in the box.
Use each word to describe something in your house.

big	fast	little	tall

_____

_ _

_____

_ _

_____

_ _

_____

_ _

_____

Write the two words that are opposites.

_____   _____

_ _ _ _ _ _ _ _ _ _ _   _ _ _ _ _ _ _ _ _ _ _

_____   _____

Big and Little

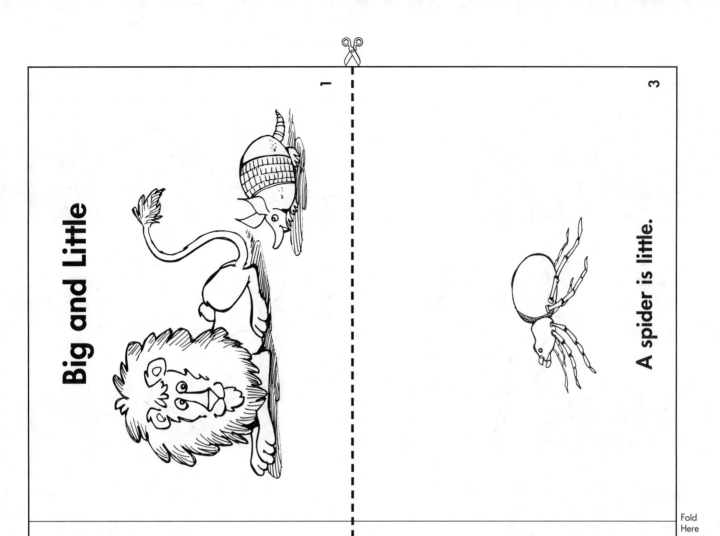

A spider is little.

Fold
Here

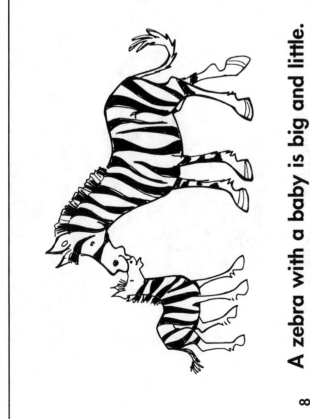

A zebra with a baby is big and little.

A giraffe is tall.

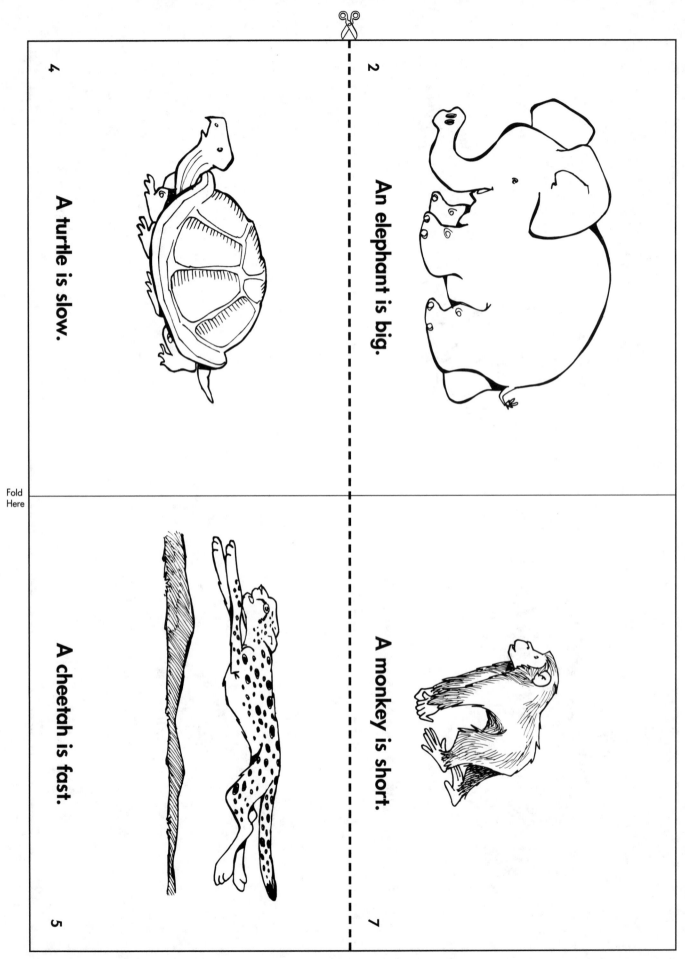

2

An elephant is big.

4

A turtle is slow.

Fold
Here

A monkey is short.

7

A cheetah is fast.

5

Name _____

At the Zoo

Comprehension: **Recalling Details**

Think about the book *Big and Little*.
Write the word that describes each animal.
Use the pictures and words to summarize the book.

_____
- - - - - - - - - - - - - - - - - - - -
_____

_____
- - - - - - - - - - - - - - - - - - - -
_____

_____
- - - - - - - - - - - - - - - - - - - -
_____

_____
- - - - - - - - - - - - - - - - - - - -
_____

_____
- - - - - - - - - - - - - - - - - - - -
_____

_____
- - - - - - - - - - - - - - - - - - - -
_____

Name_____

At the Zoo

Use the letters to make four words.

s	t	f	a

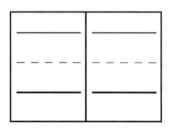

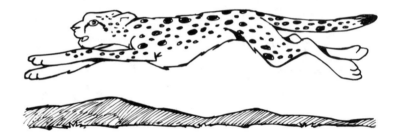

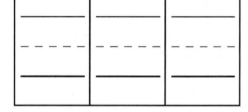

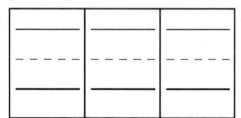

This word is the opposite of **slow**.

 Advantage Reading Grade 1 © 2004 Creative Teaching Press

Name _____

At the Zoo

Look at the map of the zoo.
Use the map to answer the questions.

What animal is next to the ? _____
_____
_____

What animal is near the ? _____

What animal is between the and the ?
_____
_____
_____
_____

What animal is across from the ? _____

Name _____

At the Zoo

You can see many animals at a zoo.
Which animal would you like to take care of?
Draw a picture of your animal.
Write two sentences to describe it.

Name _____

More Things to Do

At the Zoo

Look for these spelling patterns in newspapers or magazines: **-an, -et, -ig, -op, -ug**. Use a marker to underline the spelling pattern. See if you can change a letter to make a new word. Looking for patterns in words will help you become a better reader. Choose one or two activities from below to complete.

1 Make a picture map of your local zoo. Invent symbols or pictures for places and animals on your map. Don't forget to draw a key for your map.

2 Adopt a favorite zoo animal. Read books to find out more about the animal.

3 Use play dough to make zoo animals. Use materials such as boxes, sticks, and rocks to make a special habitat for each animal. Don't forget to make signs!

4 Make a scrapbook of zoo animals. Many of the animals come from faraway places. Find out where each animal is from.

Check out these books.

The Baby Zoo by Bruce McMillan (Scholastic)

If Everything Ever Goes Wrong at the Zoo by Mary Jean Hendrick (Voyager Books)

Little Panda: The World Welcomes Hua Mei at the San Diego Zoo by Joanne Ryder (Simon & Schuster)

Wonderful!

Good Job!

Let's go to the post office.

Name _____

Going to the Post Office

A post office is a busy place.
Draw and label four things at a post office.

What question would you ask a mail carrier?

_____

Name _____

Going to the Post Office

Phonemic Awareness: Hearing Middle Sounds

Name the pictures.
Draw a line to match pictures whose names have the same middle sound.

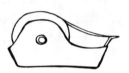

Draw two pictures that have the same middle sound as .

Name _____

Name the pictures.
Color in the boxes to show how many beats you hear.

Going to the Post Office

I hear two beats in .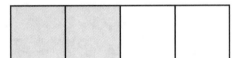

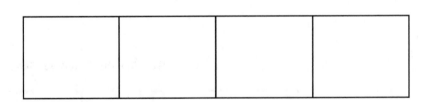

Draw and label a picture that has two beats.

Name _____

Going to the Post Office

Unscramble the letters to make words.
Write the words.
Draw a picture for each word.

k e c a
_____
- - - - - - - - - - - -
_____

a g e m
_____
- - - - - - - - - - - -
_____

e a t p
_____
- - - - - - - - - - - -
_____

f e c a
_____
- - - - - - - - - - - -
_____

Read your words.
Write a word that
rhymes with **space**.

_____
- - - - - - - - - - - -
_____

Name _____

Going to the Post Office

Read the words in the box.
Sort the words by spelling pattern.

wet	hen	jeep	feet	team
web	pea	sheep	seal	

bee	beam	ten

Read your words.
Write a word
that names
something to eat.

_____

_____

Advantage Reading Grade 1 © 2004 Creative Teaching Press

Name _____

Going to the Post Office

Unscramble the letters to make words.
Write the words.
Draw a picture for each word.

e v f i

_____
- - - - - - - - - - - - - - -
_____

b k e i

_____
- - - - - - - - - - - - - - -
_____

i n e n

_____
- - - - - - - - - - - - - - -
_____

c e m i

_____
- - - - - - - - - - - - - - -
_____

Read your words. Write a word
that rhymes with **hike**.

_____
- - - - - - - - - - - - - - -
_____

Name _____

Going to the Post Office

Read the words in the box.
Write the words that have the same long vowel sound
as 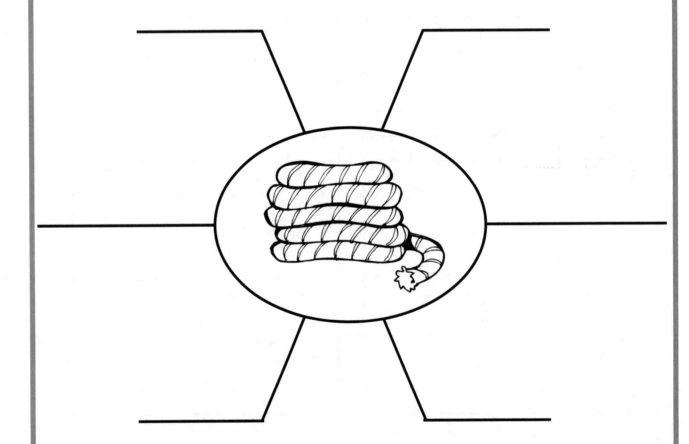.

nose	lot	rose	row	bone
box	home	doll	toe	sock

Read the words. Write a word that
names something on your face.

_____

    Advantage Reading Grade 1 © 2004 Creative Teaching Press

Name _____

Going to the Post Office

Unscramble the letters to make words.
Write the words.

| u | b | e | t | _____ |

| c | e | u | t | _____ |

| r | e | l | u | _____ |

| J | e | u | n | _____ |

| u | n | e | t | _____ |

Read your words. Write a word that
names a month of the year.

_____

Name _____

Going to the Post Office

Read each word.
Add an **e** to make a new word.
Write one more word with the same long vowel sound.

tub _____   _____

mad _____   _____

rob _____   _____

can _____   _____

pin _____   _____

Name _____

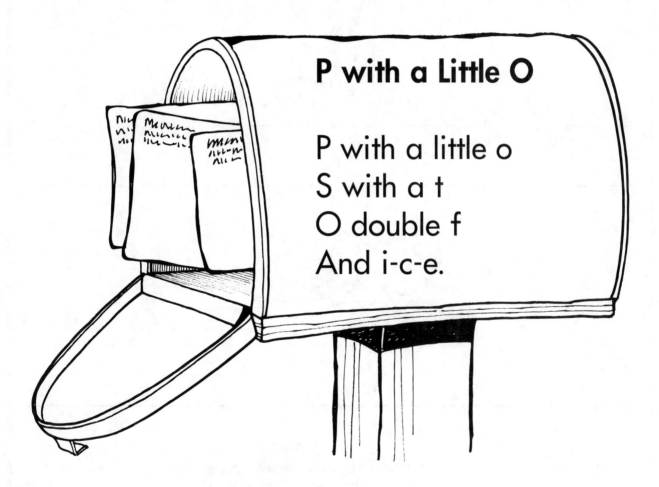

P with a Little O

P with a little o
S with a t
O double f
And i-c-e.

Read the poem again. This time read it faster.
Clap your hands to the rhythm of the poem.
Now say the poem as you write what it spells.

_____

_____

Name _____

Going to the Post Office

Look at the pictures.
Write one question about each picture.

_____

_____

_____

_____

_____

_____

56

Name _____

Going to the Post Office

Vocabulary: High-Frequency Words

Read the words in the box.
Use the words to complete the sentences.

and	he	out	look

Did you _____ in the mailbox?

Mike went _____ the door.

Will _____ mail the letter?

Mike sent a letter _____ a postcard.

Name _____

Going to the Post Office

Read the words in the box.
Choose one word.
Write and draw how you dress in that weather.

| rainy | sunny | windy |
| cloudy | snowy | stormy |

_____

- - - - - - - - - - - - - - - - - - -

_____

Write the word that begins like ⬦ .   _____

- - - - - - - - - - - - - - - - - - -

_____

    Advantage Reading Grade 1 © 2004 Creative Teaching Press

1

Time to Write

3

Mike writes a letter.
He writes another and another.

Fold
Here

"It is time to go to the post office," says Mike.

8

Mike looks out the window.
It is sunny outside.

6

4

Mike looks out the window.
It is cloudy outside.

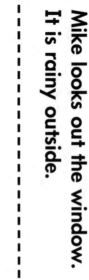

Fold
Here

2

Mike looks out the window.
It is rainy outside.

7

Mike hops on his bike.
He puts the mail in his backpack.

Mike writes a postcard.
He writes another and another.

5

Name _____

Going to the Post Office

Think about the book *Time to Write*.
Draw what happened at the beginning, middle, and end of the story.
Use the pictures to retell the book.

Beginning

▼

Middle

▼

End

Phonics: **Making Words**

Going to the Post Office

Use the letters to make four words.

| t | s | o | p |
| d | a | r | c |

This word is a compound word.

Name _____

Going to the Post Office

What happens when you mail a letter?
Use the chart to answer the questions.

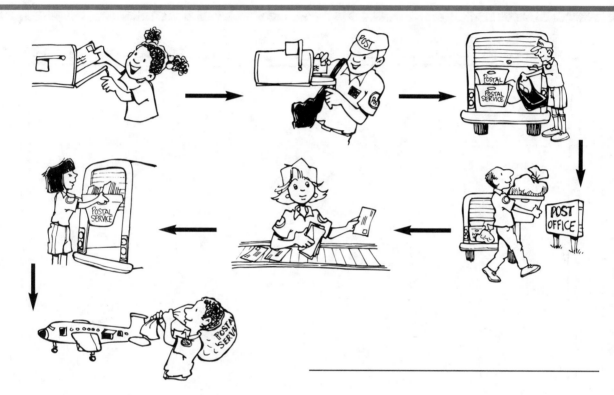

What is the girl doing? _____

Where does the take the mail?

_____

_____

What happens next? _____

Name _____

Going to the Post Office

Writing: **Descriptions**

Design a stamp.
Write a description that tells about your stamp.
Tell why your stamp is special.

_____

_ _

_____

_ _

_____

Name _____

More Things to Do

Going to the Post Office

Writing letters is a great way to put your knowledge of letter sounds and spelling patterns to work. As you write, stretch out the sounds you hear in each word. Write down the letters you hear for each sound. Think about spelling patterns you know to help write the words. Choose one or two activities from below to complete.

1. Write letters or postcards to a pen pal. Don't forget to put a stamp on your letter.

2. Start a stamp collection. Read books to find out more about the special stamps.

3. Make your own stationery. Use your thumb and a stamp pad to make thumbprints. Add details with markers to make your stationery colorful and fun!

Check out these books.

A Day With a Mail Carrier by Jan Kottke (Children's Book Press)

The Post Office Book: Mail and How It Moves by Gail Gibbons (HarperTrophy)

To the Post Office with Mama by Sue Farrell (Annick Press)

Stamp of Approval!

Wow!

Off to the park!

Name _____

Playtime at the Park

Comprehension: Prior Knowledge

Playgrounds are great places to play.
Think of things you can do at a playground.
List details in each box.

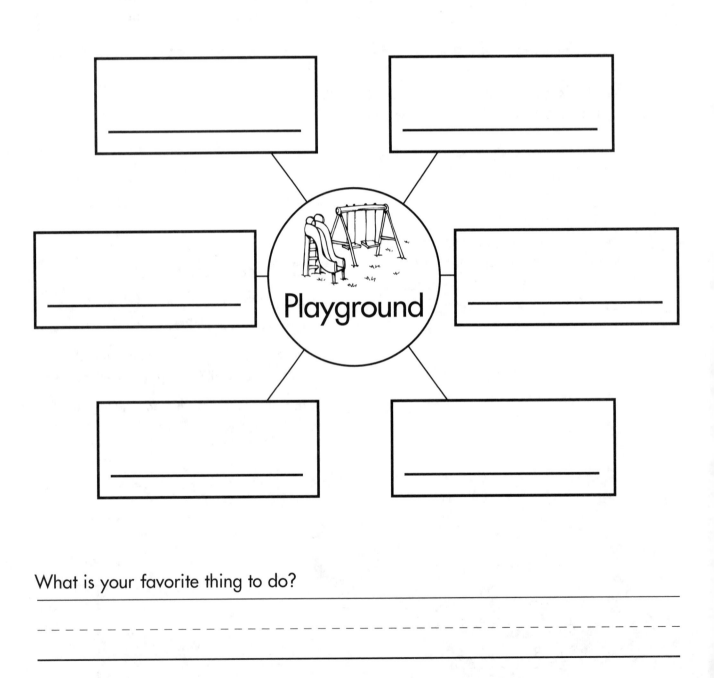

Playground

What is your favorite thing to do?

_____

_____

Name _____

Playtime at the Park

Name the pictures.
Listen to the beginning sound.
Look at the letter. Say the letter sound.
Use it at the beginning to make a new word.

  m   man

h   _____

f   _____

c   _____

s   _____

Which word rhymes with ?   _____

Name _____

Playtime at the Park

Name the pictures.
Listen to the ending sound.
Look at the letter. Say the letter sound.
Use it at the end to make a new word.

t   fat

n   _____

d   _____

d   _____

m   _____

Which word ends the same as ⬚ ?

_____

Name _____

Phonics: **Blends with l**

Playtime at the Park

Look at the letters in the box.
Use the letters to write a word that names each picture.

bl	cl	fl	pl	sl

_____ ed

_____ ate

_____ ock

_____ y

_____ ide

_____ ock

Write the two words that have the same beginning sound.

_____   _____

_____   _____

Playtime at the Park

Phonics: **Blends with s**

Look at the letters in the box.
Use the letters to write a word that names each picture.

st	sp	sm	sn	sk

_____ ail

_____ ider

_____ ile

_____ irt

_____ ake

_____ ar

Write the two words that have the same beginning sound.

_____   _____

_____   _____

   Advantage Reading Grade 1 © 2004 Creative Teaching Press

Phonics: **Blends with r**

Playtime at the Park

Look at the letters in the box.
Use the letters to write a word that names each picture.

gr	fr	tr	cr	br

_____ ick

_____ og

_____ ush

_____ uck

_____ ape

_____ ib

Write the two words that have the same ending sound.

_____ _____

_____ _____

_____ _____

Name _____

Playtime at the Park

Read the words in the box.
Sort the words that start with the same blend.

spoon	tree	spot	trip	flag
fly	train	flow		spin

_____

_____

_____

_____

_____

     Advantage Reading Grade 1 © 2004 Creative Teaching Press

Name _____

Playtime at the Park

Read the words in the box.
Write each word next to its definition.

crib	slide	snow
grape	spider	clock

Something to play on _____

It has 8 legs _____

Something cold _____

A fruit _____

Tells time _____

A baby's bed _____

Name _____

Playtime at the Park

Read each word part.
Add a blend from the box to make a word.
Write one more word with the same beginning blend.

| pl | gr | sn |
| tr | st | sl |

ip _____ _____

ap _____ _____

ane _____ _____

op _____ _____

ide _____ _____

Use one of the words to write a question.

_____

_____

Name _____

Playtime at the Park

Read the jump rope chant.
Answer the questions.

Dolly Dimple walks like this.
Dolly Dimple talks like this.
Dolly Dimple smiles like this.
Dolly Dimple throws a kiss.

Read it again.
How will you read it?   (Fast)   (Slow)

Read it again.
How will you read it?   (Big voice)   (Little voice)

Write the words that tell what Dolly Dimple does.

_____   _____

_____   _____

_____   _____

Name _____

Playtime at the Park

Look at the picture.
What details do you see?
List the details under the picture.

_____

_____

_____

_____

Write a title for the picture.

_____

_____

Name _____

Playtime at the Park

Read the words in the box.
Use the words to complete the sentences.

up	on	to	like

Do you _____ to play at the playground?

The seesaw goes _____ and down.

It is not fun _____ sit on the bench.

Let's ride _____ the merry-go-round.

Name _____

Playtime at the Park

Read the words in the box.
Write the word that tells what each character is doing.

rolls	digs	jumps
climbs	hops	runs

_____

_____

_____

_____

Use one word to describe how you like to move.

_____

_____

Playtime

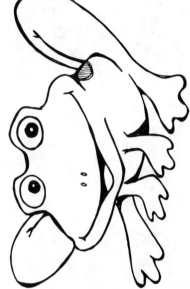

Frog climbs up a ladder.
"I like to climb," says Frog.

Fold
Here

Kerplunk!
Frog sleeps on a bench.
ZZZZZ*zzzzz*

Frog kicks a soccer ball.
"I like to kick," says Frog.

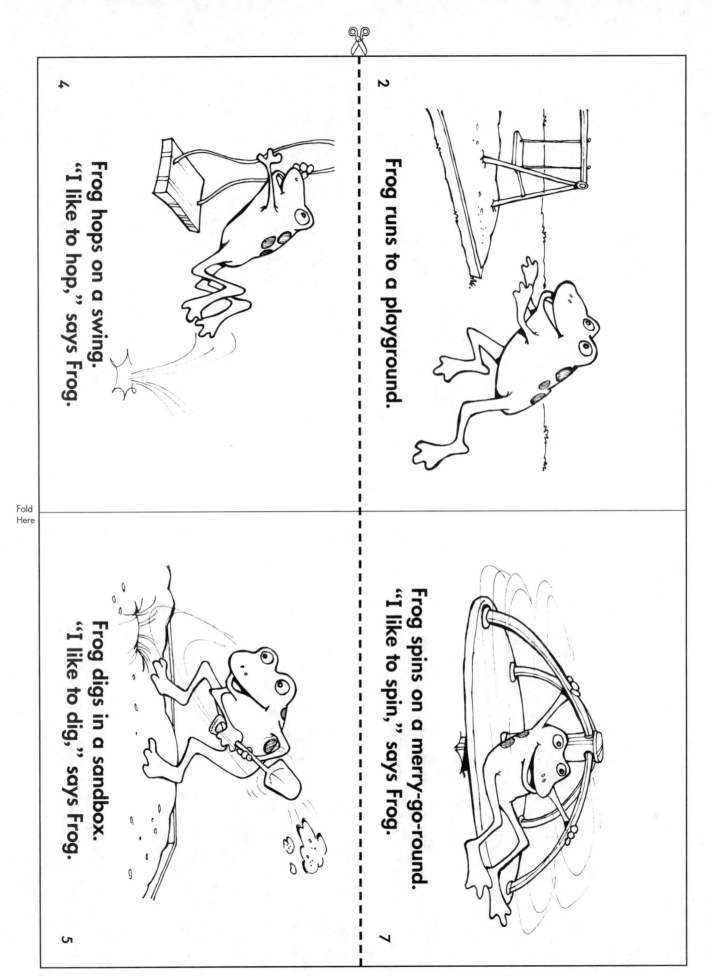

6

4

Frog hops on a swing.
"I like to hop," says Frog.

2

Frog runs to a playground.

Fold Here

Frog spins on a merry-go-round.
"I like to spin," says Frog.

Frog digs in a sandbox.
"I like to dig," says Frog.

5

7

Name _____

Playtime at the Park

Comprehension: **Cause and Effect**

Think about the book *Playtime*.
Draw what happens to Frog.
Use the pictures to retell the book.

What did Frog do?

Frog was tired because . . .

Name _____

Playtime at the Park

Use the letters to make four words.

e	s	i	d	l

This word rhymes with **ride**.

Advantage Reading Grade 1 © 2004 Creative Teaching Press

Name _____

Playtime at the Park

Read how to make monster bubbles.
Answer the questions.

Monster Bubbles

You will need:

1 dishwashing soap

$\frac{1}{2}$ corn syrup

12  water

large bucket

funnel

1. First, mix the soap, corn syrup, and water in a large bucket.

2. Then, let the mixture sit for one day.

3. Next, put the big end of the funnel into the mixture. Pull it out slowly.

4. Last, blow some monster bubbles.

Which item do you need 12 of?

_____

_____

What kind of soap do you need?

_____

_____

Write words that tell order.

_____

_____

Name _____

Playtime at the Park

Write directions for how to play a favorite game.
Use words that tell order such as **first, next,** and **last.**

_____

_ _ _ _ _ _ _ _ _ _ _ _ _ _ _ _ _ _ _ _

_____

_ _ _ _ _ _ _ _ _ _ _ _ _ _ _ _ _ _ _ _

_____

_ _ _ _ _ _ _ _ _ _ _ _ _ _ _ _ _ _ _ _

_____

_ _ _ _ _ _ _ _ _ _ _ _ _ _ _ _ _ _ _ _

_____

_ _ _ _ _ _ _ _ _ _ _ _ _ _ _ _ _ _ _ _

_____

_ _ _ _ _ _ _ _ _ _ _ _ _ _ _ _ _ _ _ _

    Advantage Reading Grade 1 © 2004 Creative Teaching Press

Name _____

More Things to Do

Playtime at the Park

When you explain how to play a new game, you need to remember all the steps. You also need to remember to put the steps in the right order. Find different kinds of directions. Look in cookbooks, craft books, and game books. Choose one or two activities from below to complete.

1 Share simple directions for how to get to a friend's house or to your school. Write the directions down. Follow your directions. Check to see if you remembered all the steps.

2 Design a playground ride. Think of a special ride you could build in your school or neighborhood playground. Decide what it looks like and make a sketch.

3 Collect favorite playground chants! Write the chants on index cards. Punch a hole in each card and put the cards on a ring.

Check out these books.

Acka Backa Boo: Playground Games from Around the World by Opal Dunn (Henry Holt & Company)

Heard It In the Playground by Allan Ahlberg (Penguin U.K.)

King of the Playground by Phyllis Reynolds Naylor (Aladdin)

Super!

Nice Job!

Let's go shopping!

Name _____

Let's Shop

You can finds lots of things in different shops.
Look at the three signs.
Write things you could buy at each shop.

Shoes	Fruits	Clothes
SHOES	APPLES	SHIRTS

Where do you like to shop?

_____

_____

Advantage Reading Grade 1 © 2004 Creative Teaching Press

Name _____

Let's Shop

Name the pictures in each row.
Listen to the beginning sounds.
Circle the pictures that have the same beginning sound.

Draw a picture of one
more thing that has the
same beginning sound
as .

Name _____

Let's Shop

Name the pictures.
Circle the pictures whose names have three sounds.

  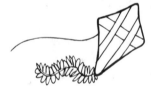

Draw a picture of one more thing that has three sounds.

88   *Advantage Reading Grade 1 © 2004 Creative Teaching Press*

Name _____

Let's Shop

Look at the pictures.
Circle the word that names each picture.

sheep
shop

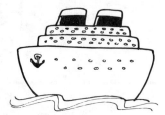

ship
shop

shoe
she

short
shirt

shell
shale

shut
shorts

What sound do
you hear at the
end of 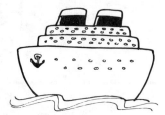 ?

_____
- - - - - - - - - - - - - - - - - -
_____

Name _____

Let's Shop

Look at the words in the box.
Unscramble the letters to make words.

chair	cheese	cherry
chin	chalk	chain

r i a h c _____

n h i c _____

c r r e h y _____

e s c e h e _____

Write a word
that has the
long e sound. _____

Name _____

Let's Shop

Look at the pictures.
Circle the word that names each picture.

well
wheel

wheat
plant

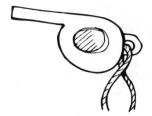
whistle
white

whiskers
white

wheelbarrow
wheel

whale
while

Read the words.
Write a word that
names something
you can find on
a cat.

_____

- - - - - - - - - - - - - - - - - -

_____

Name _____

Let's Shop

Read the words in the box.
Write each word next to its definition.

thumb	thirty	thin
thermometer		thin thump

A number _____

Opposite of fat _____

A tool _____

A finger _____

A sound _____

Let's Shop

Phonics: **Digraph kn**

Look at the words in the box.
Unscramble the letters to make words.

knee	know	knife	knock	knit

t i n k   _____

e n k e   _____

f e k n i   _____

w o n k   _____

Write the word
that is a body part.   _____

Name _____

Let's Shop

Read each word part.
Add a digraph from the box to make a word.
Write one more word with the same beginning digraph.

| kn | wh | th | sh | sl |

ug

_____   _____

is

_____   _____

ale

_____   _____

eep

_____   _____

ock

_____   _____

Use one of the words to write a sentence.

_____

_____

94   *Advantage Reading Grade 1 © 2004 Creative Teaching Press*

Name _____

Let's Shop

Read the poem with a friend.
Take turns reading each line.
Read the last two sentences together.
Read the poem several times using a different voice.

I like apples.
      I like berries.
I like pears.
      I like cherries.
I like corn.
      I like tomatoes.
I like peas.
      I like potatoes.

We like pies and ice cream too!
How about you? How about you?

Write two rhyming words from the poem.

_____   _____

_____   _____

Name _____

Let's Shop

Comprehension: Story Structure

Look at each story.
Draw the missing part.
Use the pictures to tell the stories.

Advantage Reading Grade 1 © 2004 Creative Teaching Press

Name _____

Let's Shop

Read the words in the box.
Use the words to complete the sentences.

buy	time	at	and

It is _____ for lunch.

I will meet you _____ the shop.

Do you want to _____ a hot dog?

We can have chips _____ a drink.

Name _____

Let's Shop

Read the words in the box.
Write a word that describes each picture.

cold	hard	hot	loud
quiet	soft	sour	sweet

_____

_____

_____

_____

Use one word to
describe a food
you like to eat.

_____

    Advantage Reading Grade 1 © 2004 Creative Teaching Press

Stop and Shop

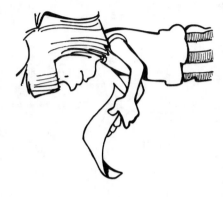

3

Shelly buys long breadsticks and small cupcakes.

Fold
Here

It's time to shop at the toy store.
Shelly buys a furry bear.
"I'll have this please."

It's time to shop at the clothing store.

2

It's time to shop at the bakery.

4

It's time to shop at the grocery store.

5

Shelly buys bumpy oranges and round grapes.

7

Shelly buys shirts with stripes and shoes with dots.

Fold
Here

100

Advantage Reading Grade 1 © 2004 Creative Teaching Press

Name _____

Let's Shop

Think about the book *Stop and Shop*.
Write what Shelly bought in each store.
Use the words to retell the story.

_____  _____

_____  _____

_____  _____

Name _____

Let's Shop

Use the letters to make four words.

s	o	e	h	s

This word is something you wear on your feet.

Name _____

Let's Shop

Use the diagram to answer the questions.

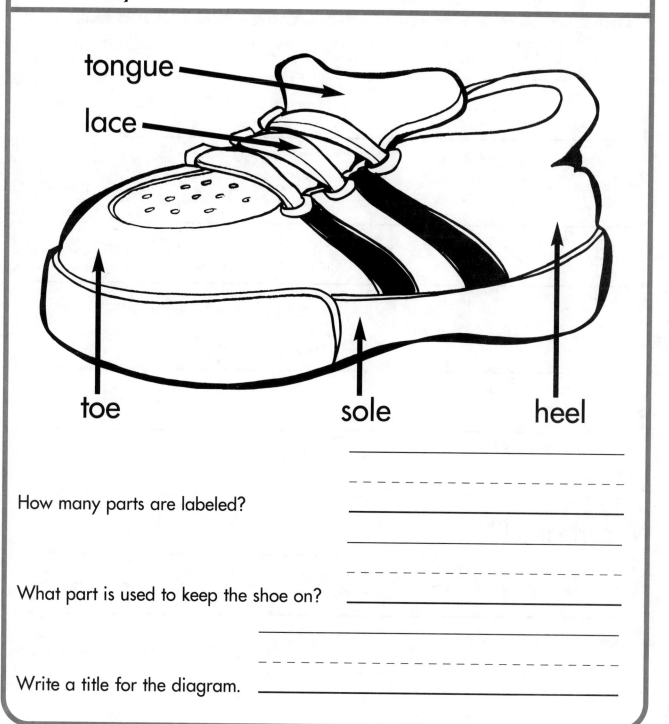

How many parts are labeled? _____

_____

What part is used to keep the shoe on? _____

_____

Write a title for the diagram. _____

Name _____

Write a riddle.
Think of something you can buy at a toy store.
Write three sentences to describe it.
Use describing words.

Let's Shop

I _____

I _____

I _____

What am I?

_____

Advantage Reading Grade 1 © 2004 Creative Teaching Press

Name _____

More Things to Do

Let's Shop

There are so many things to see when you go shopping. You will see signs everywhere. Look for words you can read on the signs. Look for little words in big words. Read the labels on cans and jars. See how many words you can read. Take a look at how the store organizes different things. Choose one or two activities from below to complete.

1 Write a shopping list before you go to a store. This will help you remember what you need to buy.

2 Organize a yard sale. Make signs for your sale. Don't forget to put price tags on your things for sale.

3 Make a wish book. Cut out pictures of things you would really like for a special day. Add a label to each picture. Put the pictures in order from the most important to the least important object.

Check out these books.

A Little Shopping by Cynthia Rylant (Simon & Schuster)

On Market Street by Arnold Lobel (Mulberry Books)

Sheep in a Shop by Nancy Shaw (Houghton Mifflin)

Signs at the Store by Mary Hill (Children's Book Press)

Magnificent!

You did it!

You reached the finish line!

Answer Key

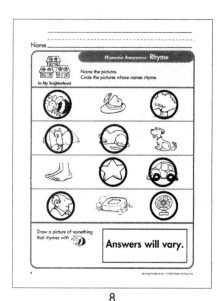

8

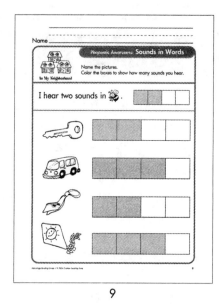

9

10

11

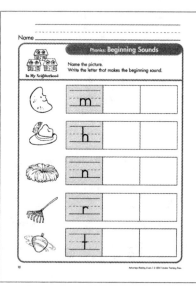

12

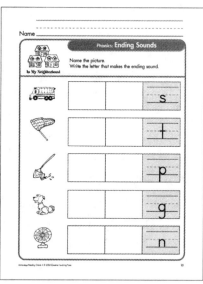

13

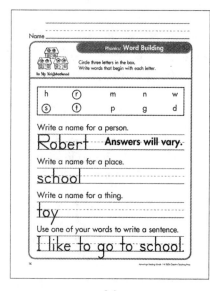

14

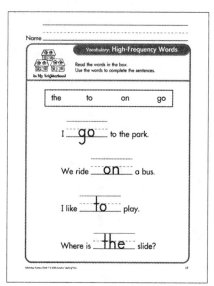

17

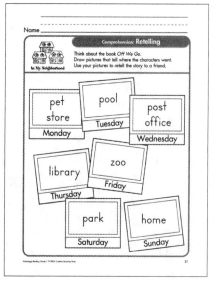

21

Phonics: Making Words

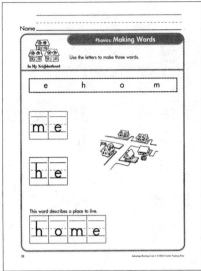

In My Neighborhood

Use the letters to make three words.

| e | h | o | m |

| m | e |

| h | e |

This word describes a place to live.

| h | o | m | e |

22

Graphic Information: Reading a Chart

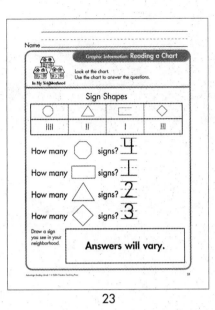

In My Neighborhood

Look at the chart.
Use the chart to answer the questions.

Sign Shapes

How many ⬡ signs? 4

How many ▭ signs? 1

How many △ signs? 2

How many ◇ signs? 3

Draw a sign you see in your neighborhood.

Answers will vary.

23

Phonemic Awareness: Beginning Sounds

At the Zoo

Name the pictures.
Draw a line to match pictures whose names have the same beginning sound.

Draw two pictures that have the same beginning sound as

**Answers will vary.
Possible drawings
include zipper, zoo, zero.**

27

Phonemic Awareness: Ending Sounds

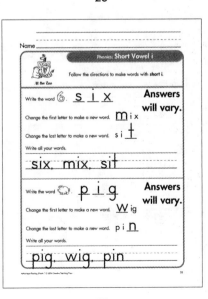

At the Zoo

Name the pictures.
Draw a line to match pictures whose names have the same ending sound.

Draw two pictures that have the same ending sound as

**Answers will vary.
Possible drawings include
whale, wheel, tool, school.**

28

Phonics: Short Vowel a

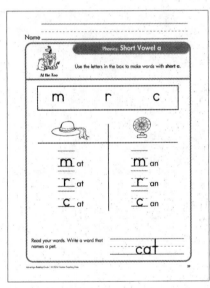

At the Zoo

Use the letters in the box to make words with **short a**.

| m | r | c |

m at	m an
r at	r an
c at	c an

Read your words. Write a word that names a pet.

cat

29

Phonics: Short Vowel e

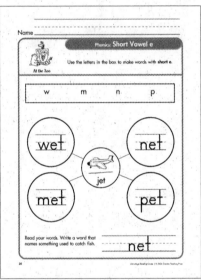

At the Zoo

Use the letters in the box to make words with **short e**.

| w | m | n | p |

wet   net

jet

met   pet

Read your words. Write a word that names something used to catch fish.

net

30

Phonics: Short Vowel i

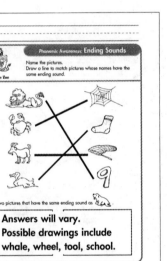

At the Zoo

Follow the directions to make words with **short i**.

Write the word 6. s i x   **Answers will vary.**

Change the first letter to make a new word. m i x

Change the last letter to make a new word. s i t

Write all your words.

six, mix, sit

Write the word 🐷 p i g   **Answers will vary.**

Change the first letter to make a new word. w ig

Change the last letter to make a new word. p i n

Write all your words.

pig, wig, pin

31

Phonics: Short Vowel o

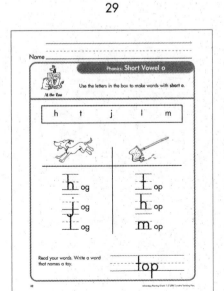

At the Zoo

Use the letters in the box to make words with **short o**.

| h | t | j | l | m |

h og	t op
j og	h op
l og	m op

Read your words. Write a word that names a toy.

top

32

Phonics: Short Vowel u

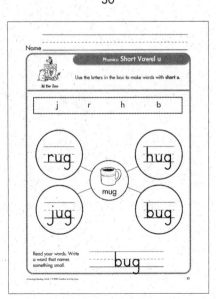

At the Zoo

Use the letters in the box to make words with **short u**.

| j | r | h | b |

rug   hug

mug

jug   bug

Read your words. Write a word that names something small.

bug

33

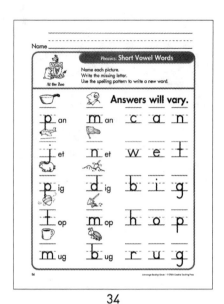

Phonics: Short Vowel Words

Name each picture.
Write the missing letter.
Use the spelling pattern to write a new word.

At the Zoo

Answers will vary.

p an   m an   c a n
j et   n et   w e t
p ig   d ig   b i g
t op   m op   h o p
m ug   b ug   r u g

34

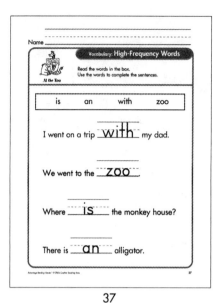

Vocabulary: High-Frequency Words

Read the words in the box.
Use the words to complete the sentences.

At the Zoo

| is | an | with | zoo |

I went on a trip **with** my dad.

We went to the **zoo** .

Where **is** the monkey house?

There is **an** alligator.

37

Comprehension: Recalling Details

Think about the book *Big and Little*.
Write the word that describes each animal.
Use the pictures and words to summarize the book.

At the Zoo

big
little
slow
fast
tall
short

41

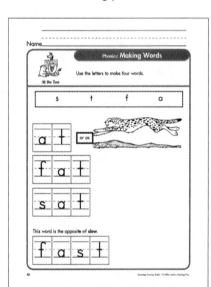

Phonics: Making Words

Use the letters to make four words.

At the Zoo

| s | t | f | a |

a t   or as
f a t
s a t

This word is the opposite of **slow**.

f a s t

42

Graphic Information: Map It!

Look at the map of the zoo.
Use the map to answer the questions.

At the Zoo

What animal is next to the ? **zebra**

What animal is near the ? **monkey**

What animal is between the and the ? **elephant**

What animal is across from the ? **monkey**

43

Phonemic Awareness: Hearing Middle Sounds

Name the pictures.
Draw a line to match pictures whose names have the same middle sound.

Going to the Post Office

Draw two pictures that have the same middle sound as .

**Answers will vary.
Possible drawings include rain, hay, train, cape.**

47

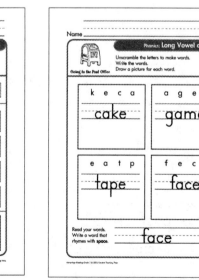

Phonemic Awareness: Syllables

Name the pictures.
Color in the boxes to show how many beats you hear.

Going to the Post Office

I hear two beats in .

Draw and label a picture that has two beats.

Answers will vary.

48

Phonics: Long Vowel a

Unscramble the letters to make words.
Write the words.
Draw a picture for each word.

Going to the Post Office

k e c a   **cake**
a g e m   **game**
e a t p   **tape**
f e c a   **face**

Read your words.
Write a word that rhymes with **space**.

face

49

Phonics: Long Vowel e

Read the words in the box.
Sort the words by spelling pattern.

Going to the Post Office

| wet | hen | jeep | feet | team |
| web | pea | sheep | seal | |

bee	beam	ten
sheep	team	wet
jeep	pea	hen
feet	seal	web

Read your words.
Write a word that names something to eat.

pea

50

Phonics: Long Vowel i

Going to the Post Office

Unscramble the letters to make words.
Write the words.
Draw a picture for each word.

e v f i	b k e i
five	bike

i n e n	c e m i
nine	mice

Read your words. Write a word that rhymes with **hike**. bike

51

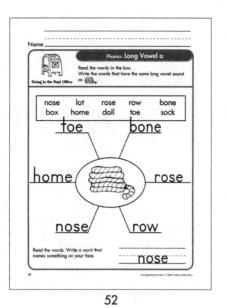

Phonics: Long Vowel o

Going to the Post Office

Read the words in the box.
Write the words that have the same long vowel sound as [mailbox].

| nose | lot | rose | row | bone |
| box | home | doll | toe | sock |

toe   bone

home   rose

nose   row

Read the words. Write a word that names something on your face. nose

52

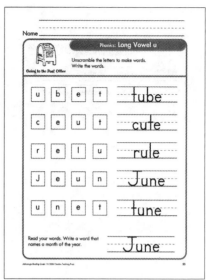

Phonics: Long Vowel u

Going to the Post Office

Unscramble the letters to make words.
Write the words.

u b e t	tube
c e u t	cute
r e l u	rule
J e u n	June
u n e t	tune

Read your words. Write a word that names a month of the year. June

53

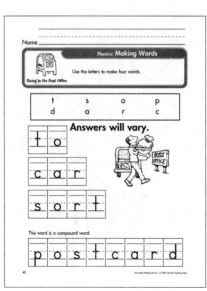

Phonics: Word Building

Going to the Post Office

Read each word.
Add an e to make a new word.
Write one more word with the same long vowel sound.

tub	tube	rule
		Answers will vary.
mad	made	say
rob	robe	toe
can	cane	rain
pin	pine	line

54

Vocabulary: High-Frequency Words

Going to the Post Office

Read the words in the box.
Use the words to complete the sentences.

| and | he | out | look |

Did you look in the mailbox?

Mike went out the door.

Will he mail the letter?

Mike sent a letter and a postcard.

57

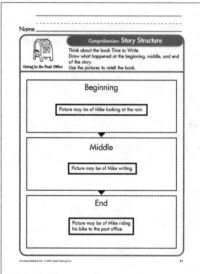

Comprehension: Story Structure

Going to the Post Office

Think about the book *Time to Write*.
Draw what happened at the beginning, middle, and end of the story.
Use the pictures to retell the book.

Beginning

Picture may be of Mike looking at the rain.

▼

Middle

Picture may be of Mike writing.

▼

End

Picture may be of Mike riding his bike to the post office.

61

Phonics: Making Words

Going to the Post Office

Use the letters to make four words.

| t | s | o | p |
| d | a | r | c |

Answers will vary.

t	o
c	a	r
s	o	r	t

This word is a compound word.

| p | o | s | t | c | a | r | d |

62

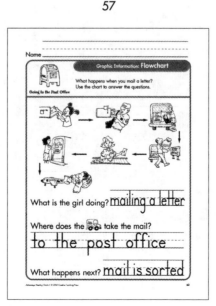

Graphic Information: Flowchart

Going to the Post Office

What happens when you mail a letter?
Use the chart to answer the questions.

What is the girl doing? mailing a letter

Where does the [truck] take the mail?
to the post office

What happens next? mail is sorted

63

Phonemic Awareness: Changing Sounds

Playtime at the Park

Name the pictures.
Listen to the beginning sound.
Look at the letter. Say the letter sound.
Use it at the beginning to make a new word.

| [mitt] | m | man |

[cat]	h	hat
[sun]	f	fun
[map]	c	cap
[hat]	s	sat

Which word rhymes with [sun]? fun

67

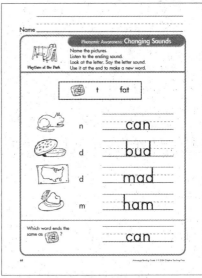

Page 68

Name _____

Phonemic Awareness: **Changing Sounds**

Playtime at the Park

Name the pictures.
Listen to the ending sound.
Look at the letter. Say the letter sound.
Use it at the end to make a new word.

| | t | fat |

	n	can
	d	bud
	d	mad
	m	ham

Which word ends the same as [ ] ? can

68

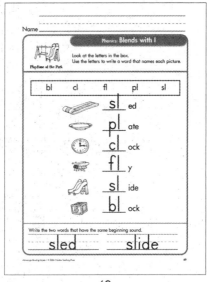

Page 69

Name _____

Phonics: **Blends with l**

Playtime at the Park

Look at the letters in the box.
Use the letters to write a word that names each picture.

| bl | cl | fl | pl | sl |

sl ed
pl ate
cl ock
fl y
sl ide
bl ock

Write the two words that have the same beginning sound.

sled   slide

69

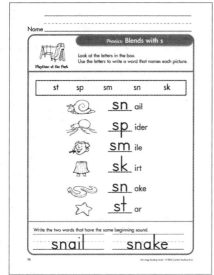

Page 70

Name _____

Phonics: **Blends with s**

Playtime at the Park

Look at the letters in the box.
Use the letters to write a word that names each picture.

| st | sp | sm | sn | sk |

sn ail
sp ider
sm ile
sk irt
sn ake
st ar

Write the two words that have the same beginning sound.

snail   snake

70

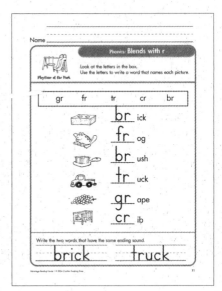

Page 71

Name _____

Phonics: **Blends with r**

Playtime at the Park

Look at the letters in the box.
Use the letters to write a word that names each picture.

| gr | fr | tr | cr | br |

br ick
fr og
br ush
tr uck
gr ape
cr ib

Write the two words that have the same ending sound.

brick   truck

71

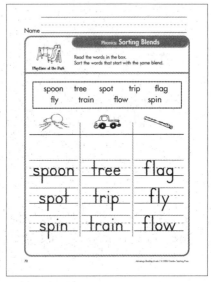

Page 72

Name _____

Phonics: **Sorting Blends**

Playtime at the Park

Read the words in the box.
Sort the words that start with the same blend.

| spoon | tree | spot | trip | flag |
| fly | train | flow | spin | |

spoon	tree	flag
spot	trip	fly
spin	train	flow

72

Page 73

Name _____

Phonics: **Reading Blends**

Playtime at the Park

Read the words in the box.
Write each word next to its definition.

| crib | slide | snow |
| grape | spider | clock |

Something to play on slide
It has 8 legs spider
Something cold snow
A fruit grape
Tells time clock
A baby's bed crib

73

Page 74

Name _____

Phonics: **Word Building**

Playtime at the Park

Read each word part.
Add a blend from the box to make a word.
Write one more word with the same beginning blend.

| pl | gr | sn |
| tr | st | sl |

Answers will vary.

ip   trip   treat
ap   snap   snore
ane   plane   plate
op   stop   stand
ide   slide   slip

Use one of the words to write a question.

Answers will vary.

74

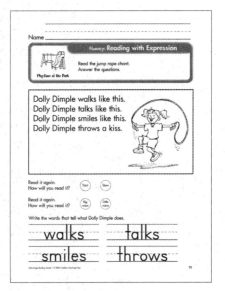

Page 75

Name _____

Fluency: **Reading with Expression**

Playtime at the Park

Read the jump rope chant.
Answer the questions.

Dolly Dimple walks like this.
Dolly Dimple talks like this.
Dolly Dimple smiles like this.
Dolly Dimple throws a kiss.

Read it again.
How will you read it? (Fast) (Slow)

Read it again.
How will you read it? (Big voice) (Little voice)

Write the words that tell what Dolly Dimple does.

walks   talks
smiles   throws

75

Page 76

Name _____

Comprehension: **Noting Details**

Playtime at the Park

Look at the picture.
What details do you see?
List the details under the picture.

jumping, swinging, digging,
climbing, playing

Write a title for the picture.

Answers will vary.

76

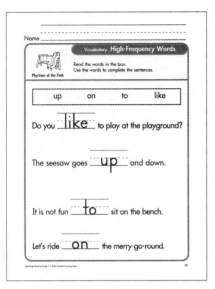

Name _____

Vocabulary: High-Frequency Words

Playtime at the Park

Read the words in the box.
Use the words to complete the sentences.

| up | on | to | like |

Do you __like__ to play at the playground?

The seesaw goes __up__ and down.

It is not fun __to__ sit on the bench.

Let's ride __on__ the merry-go-round.

77

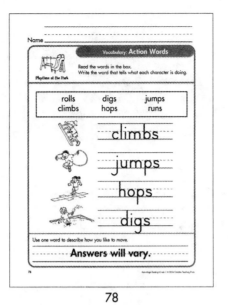

Name _____

Vocabulary: Action Words

Playtime at the Park

Read the words in the box.
Write the word that tells what each character is doing.

| rolls | digs | jumps |
| climbs | hops | runs |

__climbs__

__jumps__

__hops__

__digs__

Use one word to describe how you like to move.

Answers will vary.

78

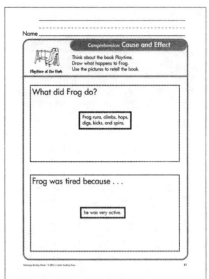

Name _____

Comprehension: Cause and Effect

Playtime at the Park

Think about the book *Playtime*.
Draw what happens to Frog.
Use the pictures to retell the book.

What did Frog do?

Frog runs, climbs, hops, digs, kicks, and spins.

Frog was tired because . . .

he was very active.

81

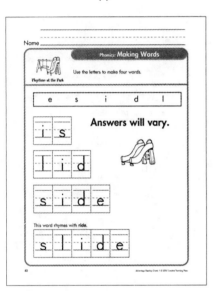

Name _____

Phonics: Making Words

Playtime at the Park

Use the letters to make four words.

| e | s | i | d | l |

Answers will vary.

i s

l i d

s i d e

This word rhymes with **ride**.

s l i d e

82

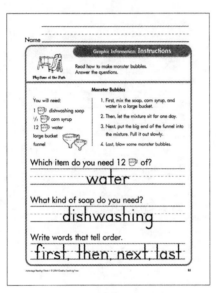

Name _____

Graphic Information: Instructions

Playtime at the Park

Read how to make monster bubbles.
Answer the questions.

Monster Bubbles

You will need:
1 dishwashing soap
1/3 corn syrup
12 water
large bucket
funnel

1. First, mix the soap, corn syrup, and water in a large bucket.
2. Then, let the mixture sit for one day.
3. Next, put the big end of the funnel into the mixture. Pull it out slowly.
4. Last, blow some monster bubbles.

Which item do you need 12 of?

__water__

What kind of soap do you need?

__dishwashing__

Write words that tell order.

__first, then, next, last__

83

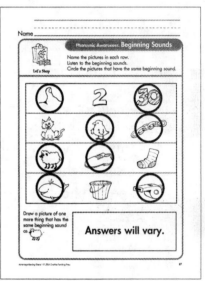

Name _____

Phonemic Awareness: Beginning Sounds

Let's Shop

Name the pictures in each row.
Listen to the beginning sounds.
Circle the pictures that have the same beginning sound.

Draw a picture of one more thing that has the same beginning sound as

Answers will vary.

87

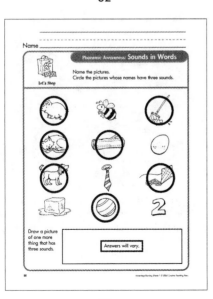

Name _____

Phonemic Awareness: Sounds in Words

Let's Shop

Name the pictures.
Circle the pictures whose names have three sounds.

Draw a picture of one more thing that has three sounds.

Answers will vary.

88

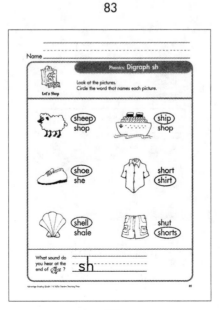

Name _____

Phonics: Digraph sh

Let's Shop

Look at the pictures.
Circle the word that names each picture.

sheep / shop

ship / shop

shoe / she

short / shirt

shell / shale

shut / shorts

What sound do you hear at the end of ?

__sh__

89

Name _____

Phonics: Digraph ch

Let's Shop

Look at the words in the box.
Unscramble the letters to make words.

| chair | cheese | cherry |
| chin | chalk | chain |

r i a h c __chair__

n h i c __chin__

c r r e h y __cherry__

e s c e h e __cheese__

Write a word that has the **long e** sound.

__cheese__

90

91

Phonics: Digraph wh

Let's Shop

Look at the pictures.
Circle the word that names each picture.

- well / **wheel**
- **wheat** / plant
- **whistle** / white
- **whiskers** / white
- **wheelbarrow** / wheel
- whale / **while**

Read the words.
Write a word that names something you can find on a cat.

whiskers

91

92

Phonics: Digraph th

Let's Shop

Read the words in the box.
Write each word next to its definition.

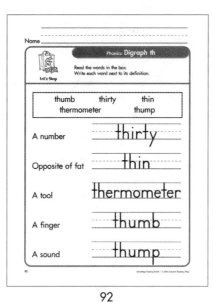

thumb	thirty	thin
thermometer		thump

- A number — thirty
- Opposite of fat — thin
- A tool — thermometer
- A finger — thumb
- A sound — thump

92

93

Phonics: Digraph kn

Let's Shop

Look at the words in the box.
Unscramble the letters to make words.

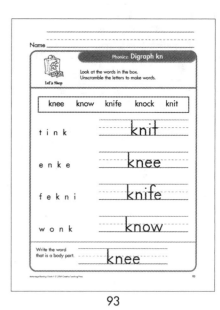

knee	know	knife	knock	knit

- t i n k — knit
- e n k e — knee
- f e k n i — knife
- w o n k — know

Write the word that is a body part. — knee

93

94

Phonics: Word Building

Let's Shop

Read each word part.
Add a digraph from the box to make a word.
Write one more word with the same beginning digraph.

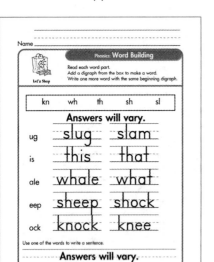

kn	wh	th	sh	sl

Answers will vary.

- ug — slug / slam
- is — this / that
- ale — whale / what
- eep — sheep / shock
- ock — knock / knee

Use one of the words to write a sentence.
Answers will vary.

94

97

Vocabulary: High-Frequency Words

Let's Shop

Read the words in the box.
Use the words to complete the sentences.

buy	time	at	and

- It is **time** for lunch.
- I will meet you **at** the shop.
- Do you want to **buy** a hot dog?
- We can have chips **and** a drink.

97

98

Vocabulary: Descriptive Words

Let's Shop

Read the words in the box.
Write a word that describes each picture.

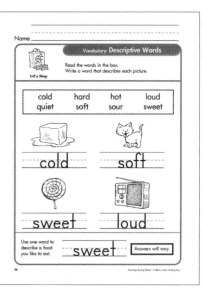

cold	hard	hot	loud
quiet	soft	sour	sweet

- cold
- soft
- sweet
- loud

Use one word to describe a food you like to eat. — sweet
Answers vary.

98

101

Comprehension: Noting Details

Let's Shop

Think about the book *Stop and Shop*.
Write what Shelly bought in each store.
Use the words to retell the story.

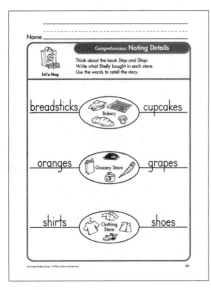

- breadsticks — Bakery — cupcakes
- oranges — Grocery Store — grapes
- shirts — Clothing Store — shoes

101

102

Phonics: Making Words

Let's Shop

Use the letters to make four words.

s	o	e	h	s

Answers will vary.

- s o
- s h e
- h o s e

This word is something you wear on your feet.

- s h o e s

102

103

Graphic Information: Diagram

Let's Shop

Use the diagram to answer the questions.

- tongue
- lace
- toe
- sole
- heel

How many parts are labeled? — five
What part is used to keep the shoe on? — lace
Write a title for the diagram. — Parts of a Shoe

103